At the Construction Site

Look, a Mixer!

By Julia Jaske

 A mixer makes concrete
in a truck.

A mixer pours concrete
in a truck.

 A mixer makes concrete
for a sidewalk.

A mixer pours concrete
for a sidewalk.

A mixer makes concrete
for a road.

A mixer pours concrete
for a road.

 A mixer makes concrete
for a building.

A mixer pours concrete
for a building.

 A mixer makes concrete
for a house.

A mixer pours concrete
for a house.

A mixer makes concrete
for a bridge.

A mixer pours concrete for a bridge.

Word List

mixer	sidewalk	house
concrete	road	bridge
truck	building	

A mixer makes concrete in a truck.

A mixer pours concrete in a truck.

A mixer makes concrete for a sidewalk.

A mixer pours concrete for a sidewalk.

A mixer makes concrete for a road.

A mixer pours concrete for a road.

A mixer makes concrete for a building.

A mixer pours concrete for a building.

A mixer makes concrete for a house.

A mixer pours concrete for a house.

A mixer makes concrete for a bridge.

A mixer pours concrete for a bridge.

CHERRY BLOSSOM PRESS

Published in the United States of America by Cherry Lake Publishing Group
Ann Arbor, Michigan
www.cherrylakepublishing.com

Photo Credits: © GodFatherMan/Shutterstock, cover, 1, 14; © chomplearn/Shutterstock, back cover; © Philip Lange/Shutterstock, 2; © weerastudio/Shutterstock, 3; © ungvar/Shutterstock, 4; © ungvar/Shutterstock, 5; © Dizfoto/Shutterstock, 6; © Bannafarsai_Stock/Shutterstock, 7; © AleksNT/Shutterstock, 8; © Kateryna Mashkevych/Shutterstock, 9; © Aleksandr Lupin/Shutterstock, 10; © Angurt/Shutterstock, 11; © momo3oki/Shutterstock, 12; © jennyt/Shutterstock, 13

Cherry Blossom Press is an imprint of Cherry Lake Publishing Group.

Library of Congress Cataloging-in-Publication Data

Names: Jaske, Julia, author.
Title: Look, a mixer! / by Julia Jaske.
Description: Ann Arbor, Michigan : Cherry Lake Publishing, [2021] | Series:
    At the construction site
Identifiers: LCCN 2021007855 (print) | LCCN 2021007856 (ebook) | ISBN
    9781534188204 (paperback) | ISBN 9781534189607 (pdf) | ISBN
    9781534191006 (ebook)
Subjects: LCSH: Concrete mixers—Juvenile literature.
Classification: LCC TA439 .J36 2021 (print) | LCC TA439 (ebook) | DDC
    624.1/8340284—dc23
LC record available at https://lccn.loc.gov/2021007855
LC ebook record available at https://lccn.loc.gov/2021007856

Printed in the United States of America
Corporate Graphics